Chardonnay Socialist

AND OTHER RADIO POEMS

Graeme Johnstone

Chardonnay Socialist and Other Radio Poems
Copyright © 2020 by Graeme Johnstone
978-0-6488619-4-2

Published by G. & E. Johnstone. All rights reserved. No part of this publication may be reproduced in any manner whatsoever, or stored in a retrieval system or transmitted in any form or by any means, electronic, mechanical, photocopying, recording or otherwise, without the prior written permission of the author, except in the case of brief quotations embodied in critical articles or reviews. Please do not participate in or encourage the piracy of copyrighted materials in violation of authors' rights. Purchase only authorized editions.

The publisher and author assume no responsibility or liability whatsoever on the behalf of any purchaser or reader of this material. Any perceived slight of specific people or organizations is unintentional. While all attempts have been made to verify information provided in this publication, neither the author nor the publisher assumes any responsibility for errors, omissions or contrary interpretation of the subject matter herein.

A special thank you

My thanks to musical genius Pete Sullivan for suggesting I approach 88.3 Southern FM with a program idea; to station guru Petar Tolich for taking it on board and helping it flourish; to Leanne Cutler and Paul Goethel for their thorough professionalism and joyful camaraderie as 'Friday Magazine' co-hosts; to Pauline O'Brien for her encouragement in putting this collection together; and to my inspired wife Elsie who regularly suggests topics for poems, always proves invaluable in helping pull projects like this together, and - after I fall out of bed every Friday morning at 5.30 in order to write a piece - displays an innate, unerring ability to go straight back to sleep.

Contents

FOREWORD 1

THE POEMS 3

    Chardonnay Socialist 4

    Inside the great man's head 6

    The boofheads rule, but why? 9

    Kim and Donald compare styles 13

    Cheap suit, cheap cut, cheap trick 15

    Could it get any crazier? 17

    My kingdom for a dunny roll 20

    After Tom Hanks, who's next? 22

    The ABC of revenge 24

    The Big Bang Theory, in reverse 27

    Learning how to bob and weave 30

    Obsession with the 'A' Club 32

    After-dark questions fit for a Queen 34

    An idea, Your Majesty, from Sir John 36

    Heading north to save the day 39

    The beginning of the end for Facebook? 42

    Clap, clap, it's the ScoMo Rap 44

    PNG takes them all for a ride 47

    Appeals are rarely appealing 50

    A cold, black heart on display 52

Catching up with old what's-his-name 54
Here's your visa, ma Cherie 56
Black holes and other devices 58
Travels with Smiley ScoMo and Baleful Bill 60
When hopes and dreams go up in flames 63
How the unlosable was lost 68
Party for some, agony for others 70
All in our own drone zone 72
Someone's got inside my fridge 74
It began with the Three 'Wise' Men 76
Swim for freedom 79
Heavy is the knock at the door 82
Ice melt is a serious business 84
The highs and highs of being a stockbroker 86
Duty to the shareholder 88
You can trust me, I'm a banker 90
What happened to Sam? 93
Pissed off at the petrol pump 96
Christopher? He's doing just Pyne 98
Mars? Been there, ruined that 101
Donald out-tweets Malcolm 104

ABOUT THE AUTHOR 106

ABOUT THE RADIO PROGRAM 108

MORE BOOKS BY GRAEME JOHNSTONE 109

CHARDONNAY SOCIALIST — *And Other Radio Poems*

FOREWORD

In search of that matching word

A poem is a beautiful thing. It stretches the creator's skills. It can jump from tragedy to humour within a couple of lines. It fills the listener with anticipation of things about to rhyme.

That's me, an old fashioned poet who writes in rhyming couplets, three-line stanzas, all the classic techniques. I have tried the more modern approach - where rhyming appears to have gone out the window - but always the music man in me emerges and I rise to the challenge. Sometimes there is a little bit of squeezing or syllable bending, and occasionally I employ several modes within a work, but I generally stick to the object of classic verse.

A Chardonnay Socialist is defined as 'a person who espouses Socialist ideals while enjoying a wealthy and luxurious lifestyle.'

That's me, too.

Not one of stratospheric riches, I hasten to add. Not like those entertainers, film stars, artists, musicians and other billionaires bemoaning the experiences of the less fortunate. But I readily admit I have, along with my wife and family, enjoyed a lovely life in a very comfortable home in a beautiful bayside suburb once described as a 'quiet middle-class backwater.'

Still, I don't believe that should disqualify me from commenting on the world's inequalities. Oh no. I love to offer an opinion!

I have done so in my long career as a newspaper and magazine journalist, and for the last five years as the host of *Friday Magazine*, a news and interviews radio program on 88.3 Southern FM. Every Friday morning I leap out of bed at 5.30 to write a poem in time for the show going to air at 9 o'clock.

Very often the subject is what I see as an unjustness in life and the heaving mass of greedy capitalism that has caused it all - a somewhat delicious irony considering that the radio station is based in Melbourne's upmarket beachside suburb of Brighton, about twenty minutes' drive from home. In fact, the opening poem, *Chardonnay Socialist,* explores that glorious conflict.

A companion selection, more about lifestyle and personal matters, is available in *OK Boomer and other radio poems*. As with that book, I have included in this selection the broadcast date and, where necessary, an introduction to each poem to set the time and background so you can comfortably plunge into it.

I hope you get as much pleasure reading these works as I did writing and broadcasting them.

Now, having eased my conscience and solved all the world's problems, where's that bottle of wine ..?

- Graeme Johnstone.

CHARDONNAY SOCIALIST   *And Other Radio Poems*

The Poems

Chardonnay Socialist

Broadcast August 14, 2020

All hail the Chardonnay Socialist
A faux Communist notionalist
Who bleeds for those who struggle
And are victims of dark forces

He bravely backs their case
In every battle that they face
Whether it's lack of decent housing
Or cuts in social resources

He vents his white-hot rage
In the letters pages of 'The Age'
Condemning Government leaders
And fat-cat bureaucrats

And attacks lacklustre pensions
And JobSeeker suspensions
And the appalling lack of heating
In those tiny council flats

It's a humane commission
A Bayside 'Bolshie' mission
To balance the unequal treatment
Meted out to whites and blacks

CHARDONNAY SOCIALIST *And Other Radio Poems*

Taking the side of all Asians
And varying sorts of Caucasians
And phoning in on talk-back
To say he has their backs

And is their white knight
Assisting their great fight
To lift them out of 'povo'
And give life a red-hot shot

Why, only yesterday
He had a lassie down his way
Polishing his Bentley
And painting the deck on the yacht

And 'tho she did as asked
About half way through the task
She said she was from a suburb
That had something of a 'name'

So our man kept a watchful eye
And had his Doberman sit nearby
Well, it's hard to know who to trust
Much less to apportion blame

Still, at the end of the day
He felt he could honestly say
He'd done his best
To help her fill her belly

He's no cheating skiver
Why, he paid her off with a fiver
And then poured himself
A glass of Hunter Valley …

Inside the great man's head

In a rare moment, Australia's warring politicians united to honour the passing of four-time Prime Minister, Bob Hawke, just two days before the 2019 election.
Broadcast May 17, 2019.

What an astonishing life the great man led
So, how would it be to sneak inside that head?
And stroll around the brain that guided his walk and talk
The driving force of Robert James Lee Hawke

Look, this drawer here is marked with one word, 'Vision'
Which amongst leaders today has largely gone missing
He could see the future, determine which was the way
To make things better, no matter how hard the fray

And here is its partner, that over the years flourished
See, that sturdy box boldly marked 'Courage'
The way he took risks left us all in awe
But he knew he had to change all that went before

This cupboard is special, his personal favourite
'Consensus' he's marked it, and let's all savour it
Get together and sort out our differences
We can all be judge and jury and witnesses

As long as we get there in the end
Then go to the next challenge around the bend
No matter what was happening in our ever-changing world
The idea was to have a go, give it a whirl

CHARDONNAY SOCIALIST *And Other Radio Poems*

What's hanging over there? That's worthy of note
That's Bob's special garb, his larrikin's coat
He could don at will, and walk amongst us all
And have the lowest of the low held within his thrall

But then mix with the haves, and the top end of town
And even the ones poncing round in a crown
Whether a person was anonymous or revelling in fame
Bob never looked phased, treated them all the same

Now, does anyone want to open those drawers?
The ones dented and scratched and boldly marked 'Flaws'?
Ah, let's not go there on this poignant day
He admitted to them all, what else can you say?

Not for him to hide his temper and indiscretions
He talked of the women, the drink, the punting sessions
But instead of running the nation in an alcoholic fog
He knew that to do it right, he had to give up the grog

Don't touch that case marked 'Family' and 'Hazel'
We know how he was rarely at the kitchen table
Yet, as he roamed far and wide spreading cheer
He somehow became the Father of the Year!

That file marked 'Clem and Ellie' is worth noting
His Minister Dad and devoted Mum were, oh, so doting
They gave him surety, love, values and ideals
The ability to lead, and, yes, the compassion that heals

It's time to go. There is an election at large
He'll be sorry to miss it; they might get back in charge
But wait! Look, see? Down the hall?
What's that hanging proudly on the wall?

Ahh, remember them? He's had them framed!
You gotta love him; not for him to be shamed
The ultimate symbol of the Bob Hawke credo
His Labor Party Conference Speedos …

CHARDONNAY SOCIALIST — *And Other Radio Poems*

The boofheads rule, but why?

It's intriguing how nations elect as their leader an A-type, big dog with no emotional intelligence, and then let him march the country into conflict.
Broadcast September 22, 2017.

Can someone tell me
Why do we let the boofheads rule our world?
Why do we vote 'em in and let their bullying flag unfurl?

Why do we believe their promises of goodness and love?
Some boasting they come with guidance from above
And how they will pursue justice and peace
But we know when they get in
All they'll do is release
The dogs of war
And their inner beast

One session with the Generals
Is what changes their course
The old military school
Still leads the civil horse
Like playground thugs
So cruel and so coarse

We don't stand up to their power and will
Their devious pleasure to chase and to kill
No matter what a new leader will implore
These five-star tin-hats keep pushing for war

    While the silent bankers
    Sell guns and chase oil
    It breaks your heart
    It makes your blood boil

Even the lady with the flower behind her ear
Who we thought was the one to end all fear
But stuck between a rock and a hard place
She's made the same predictable about-face

And oh, the catch cries to camouflage the horror!
    'We bring democracy'
    What a joke
    'It's a new world order'
    A pig in a poke
    'Mission accomplished!'
    To soon, he spoke

    Now it's 'kicking the can down the road'
    No attempt to lighten the load
    A shrill voice from a cold, black heart
    The finger on the button, ready to start
    The program that will totally destroy
    Kill every child, smash every toy

CHARDONNAY SOCIALIST *And Other Radio Poems*

And us Down Under?
We toady along
We stand shoulder to shoulder
Showing we're loyal and strong

Both sides of the House
Doing what they're told
As meek as a mouse
Don't dare to be bold
And stand up and say
'This US policy
'Is not the solution
'It's the whole damn problem
'Based on fighting and shooting'

Instead, we invite them in
For the shroud of protection
Bow down before them
A gross genuflection

They gleefully say thanks
And go behind guarded walls
Shut everyone out and make all the calls
That'll make us a target
What a load of balls

Training exercises on people's front doors
Nuclear missiles on European floors
'This spot's American now, no longer yours'
Haven't they learnt from years before?

The carnage and destruction of the Vietnam War?
Or for that matter, all the ones before
The lunacy of Iraq, crime after crime
Based on information presented at the time

It's this interfering in other people's lives that's the blight
Going half way round the world looking for a fight
'To protect the interests of us and our allies'

Yair, that'd be right
Time for us to stand up
And change the tone
And make our mantra
'Let's look after our own'

CHARDONNAY SOCIALIST — *And Other Radio Poems*

Kim and Donald compare styles

Donald Trump tries stunts that more traditional presidents would not dare contemplate, such as meeting up with Kim Jong-Un. But maintaining focus is another matter.
Broadcast March 1, 2019.

In Hanoi they agreed to meet up
Trump and Kim, to dine and sup
The place was so charming and pretty
Don thought he was still in Atlantic City

'We flew here in the Number One can
'To talk about the big tariff log-jam
'Tell me, were the States here before
'In some sort of, like, major war ..?'

Then carefully looking around
He stooped and measured up the ground
Saying, 'Kim, here's my opening thought
'What a perfect place for a golf resort!'

'Nah,' said Kim, 'forget all that, Don
'Let's get the real discussions on
'If I end our threatening missile feud
'Will you then sell us some Yankee food?'

'Sure,' said Don. 'I'll cut to the chase
'And talk about trade and the arms race
'But, first, I have a feeling in my gut
'That you've had yourself a new haircut!'

13

'It's so sharp and smooth up each side
'I see you sport it with so much pride
'To the point it's almost envy I harbour
'Have you got yourself a specialist barber?'

'Here,' said Kim, 'I'll lend you my man
'If a new hair style will help with your plan
'To rule America with might and power
'Turning the whole place into one Trump Tower'

'Tempting,' said Don, 'but with gravity laws
'If he cuts my hair to look just like yours
'There won't be enough to flip and flop
'And pile it all together way up on top

'Between you and me, Mister Kim
'Up on the crown, I'm just a little bit thin
'And when you're in a job called POTUS
'You need to cover up so no-one will notice'

'Y-e-e-s,' said Kim, and there the talks ended
They'd broken the chain and could not mend it
Losing trust and belief and becoming territorial
Not over trade or bombs, but things tonsorial

Don went home and onto the next thing
A warning coming from an underling
'I'm afraid, Mr President, there's an ill-wind blowin''
'Put on this hat, here comes Cyclone Cohen …'

CHARDONNAY SOCIALIST — *And Other Radio Poems*

Cheap suit, cheap cut, cheap trick

From the moment he burst on the scene, Boris Johnson has always attracted attention. As his ascension to the Prime Ministerial throne drew nearer, people were left to ask, 'How?'
Broadcast July 5, 2019.

I'm feeling jealous
Just a tiny bit callous
I have a case of the covetous horrors

With envy I'm green
Venting my spleen
I wish I had a hair cut like Boris!

Oh, I saw him last night
On TV, such a sight
Coming up to a reporter, he startled her

She recoiled in fright
Because it looked like
He'd had his hair cut by a combined harvester

That's the man's mark
In the light or dark
As a leader he is a committed diversionist

He'll soon be the boss
But does he give a toss?
No, he dresses like a crumpled old journalist

But while he shuffles round
All over London town
In a suit made from a bit of old schmutter

It's conservatives he seeks
The way he speaks
With just a hint of the public school stutter

And here's another thing
He's descended from a king
You could hardly say that makes him common

To put things in the frame
Here's his full name
Alexander Boris de Pfeffel Johnson

So, one way or the other
Worried sisters and brothers
He says he will fix Brexit within a week

What a time we're in
Breath slowly in
Waiting on the master of 'decrepit chic'

CHARDONNAY SOCIALIST   *And Other Radio Poems*

Could it get any crazier?

Donald Trump decided to chase up dirt on his presidential opponent Joe Biden. So who did he go to? The Ukrainian leader, who had the perfect pre-politics career.
Broadcast October 4, 2019.

I'm in a state of confusion
My temple is contusing
And jangling both sides of my brain

It gets crazier and crazier
And just a little bit hazier
With Trump calling on that guy from Ukraine

Was it a form of treason?
Or done for good reason?
Was he trying things socioeconomic?

Talk about chew the bone
At the other end of the phone
Was a bloke who was once a stand-up comic!

Was this the ultimate skit?
More madness than of wit
With Don saying he's got nothing to be hiding

He says it won't hurt
Chasing up a little dirt
On his opponent, dear old Joe Biden

Oh, no need for that
Forget that tit-for-tat
Here's some election manna from heaven

Trump may be aging
And constantly out-raging
But soon Biden will turn seventy-seven!

Oh, Joe, give it away
Go lie down in the hay
Like a good old-fashioned Delawarean

You think it's your turn
But our future concern
Is being run by an octogenarian!

While this all sounds fraught
Impeaching will come to naught
It'll be a great Opposition blunder

Even if does get to trial
Trump'll get off by a mile
The Democrats do not have the numbers

And an interesting sideshow
What an absolute mind blow
Made us all look puzzled up to the sky

CHARDONNAY SOCIALIST *And Other Radio Poems*

It's enough to bewilder
The old nation builder
Alexander Downer, a left-leaning spy???

Just one more thing
In this mad ball of string
Trump phoned his Man Made of Titanium

ScoMo said, 'Oh no.
'That's an area we no-go
'Won't tell what's inside this cranium'

Whaddya expect?
For him to be direct?
And tell you exactly what it all means?

Did you know this is the case?
Titanium is the base
Of implants, prostheses and smoke screens ...

My kingdom for a dunny roll

How rapidly COVID-19 spread, arousing those two most basic instincts
- fear and greed.
Broadcast March 6, 2020.

It's a worrying development
Out of this virus caper
Everyone's gone stir crazy
Seeking out dunny paper

All the shelves are empty
Standing so bare and cold
The panacea for your derriere
Is now worth more than gold

People who've missed out
Charge wild-eyed around
Wrestling successful shoppers
Onto the car-park ground

Why is there such a fuss?
Why so much searing panic?
Why seek out the Sorbent
In a rush that's Satanic?

It's just like the bushfires
Their own weather they form
Fear has begotten frenzy
Producing a wild 'schmitt' storm

CHARDONNAY SOCIALIST *And Other Radio Poems*

It's a Dunny Nuclear Winter
Your very own moon eclipse
Taken out of your comfort zone
A Zombie Bum Apocalypse

Us 'OK Boomers' had
A solution for all ages
On a nail on the dunny wall
The good old Yellow Pages

Or the Dun & Bradstreet
Or the back page of The Argus
Now, that'd get us over
Our posterior catharsis

So look to your own shelves
Avoid this lunatic craze
No doubt somewhere you've got
A couple of old Melways

Or a catalogue from Aldi
That'll finish your journey
Or a JB Hifi or a Spotlight
Or a good old Dan Murphy

I hear what you're saying
Getting whingey and whiney
You reckon that for your bum
They're too glossy and shiny

There is another solution
Stepping away from this affray
I'm off to the plumbers
To buy a brand new bidet …

After Tom Hanks, who's next?

COVID-19 knows no bounds, impacting on all levels of society, even a much-loved man universally recognized for his heroics. On the big screen, that is.
Broadcast March 13, 2020.

So, Tom Hanks has got the virus
That simply cannot be right
He spent years isolated on an island
Without another person in sight

And he landed that plane in 'Sully'
Saved 'Apollo 13' after a thump
And look at all the things he survived
When playing 'Forrest Gump'

If anything was gonna get him
And I don't mean a bull to gore him
It was when he was in 'The Da Vinci Code'
And we all nearly died of boredom

So, this is a disturbing shock
If it affects such a movie hero
Next thing you'll be telling me
It's gonna hit Robert De Niro

Or maybe Sylvester Stallone
Knocking 'Rocky' right down flat
Or even Arnold Schwarzenegger
Perhaps this time he won't 'be back'

CHARDONNAY SOCIALIST *And Other Radio Poems*

See, the thing that is a worry
For stars of screen and stage
A rather common theme
Is that they are of a certain age

Now my plans are ruined
For a project that had consumed me
Writing it before the virus
The ultimate tough guy movie

It would have been a ripper
About to put some film in the can
About a chocolate-eating castaway boxing pilot astronaut hit-man …

The ABC of revenge

Coalition Governments loathe the ABC and will take any opportunity to make life difficult for the national broadcaster.
Broadcast July 3, 2020.

I cannot go on
Not worth staying alive
If the ABC news is axed
From seven forty-five

It marks my morning
Sets up the day ahead
It trumpets, 'You fat bastard
'Get your arse out of bed'

It also sets the poser
'What should I do?
'Stay in bed and listen
'Or get up for the loo?'

Trouble is, once you're up
The spell is broken
And while searching for your jocks
You hear just token

Reports of the events happening around the nation
And beyond our shores where our fascination
With China and America and Britain knows no bounds
As they rattle their sabres on the sparsest of grounds

CHARDONNAY SOCIALIST *And Other Radio Poems*

And what about the virus?
What's the latest on that?
And the heated Middle East
Full of death and combat?

And what's with the footy?
Is it going ahead?
And at those fast-food outlets
Is there more blood to be shed?

The nation has relied
On this bulletin for years
Totally tuned to it
With heart and soul as well as ears

People in units and houses and milking sheds
And factories and bakeries and around hospital beds
And driving their cars heading for the day's toil
How can they survive without the good oil?

The Government says, 'But there has been no cuts
'This angry backlash is driving us nuts
'The ABC is cashed up to its armpits
'And they'd get a shed-load more if they weren't such Marxists
'All schooled in the words of Trotsky and Lenin
'And carrying on about Iraq and Yemen
'And trying to tear our great leadership down
'Saying we're in the thrall of the top end of town
'It's up to them to cut their cloth to suit
'And if it means a news spot gets the boot
'Well, that's their decision, they have to wear it
'We say everything must be judged on its merit'

So soon the familiar trumpets will no longer blow
Replaced with more minutes of Sammy's brekkie show
Surely they could stretch things beyond the limits
Why the seven o'clock bulletin already lasts 10 minutes

CHARDONNAY SOCIALIST — *And Other Radio Poems*

The Big Bang Theory, in reverse

There were some disturbing Cold War parallels when the newly-elected Trump Administration opened up dialogue with North Korea. Broadcast April 28, 2017.

What are we doing now?
What are we trying to prove?
Why are some so keen
And forcing us to move

Into a state of hyper-madness
At an unbelievable cost
By picking on a nation
That they want to stop

From colourfully marching
Through its own town square?
Showing off its rockets?
Waving banners in the air?

Why is the virtuous West
So criminally obsessed
With pushing and prodding them
To set off a nuclear mess?

By blowing up the planet
With the Big Bang in reverse
And get us all carted away
In an atomic–powered hearse

The theory says it all began
Thirteen billion years ago
When a tiny solo particle
Quietly began to glow

With a glorious explosion
Space and time evolved
Galaxies were spun off
Our little Earth revolved

Via sweat and exhortation
We've got things to a stage
Despite the occasional problem
We've created an amazing age

But there's one crazy mob
A mighty super-power
The face of Armageddon
Cruel and dank and dour

They have to have their way
Full of invective and of bile
Hating the rocket man
And his hair in a quirky style

They say, 'Don't let him in
'He can't join our club
'It's for us to determine
'If he can have a rocket or a sub'

So tho' he's done not much
Except hurl the odd spear
They paint him as a rogue state
For all the world to fear

CHARDONNAY SOCIALIST *And Other Radio Poems*

Our PM stirred the pot
With Vice-President Pence
Who warned one and all
'We cannot sit on the fence'

Julie rattled his cage
Kim said, 'Give it a rest
'Something nasty'll hit you
'If you keep poking my nest'

Will Kim back down?
Will he be the first to blink?
As Russia did with JFK?
Hard to know what to think

Or will he go for the jugular
Refusing to bow and buckle
And blow us all away
Taking us down with a chuckle

Ah, but will the West get in first?
And who will push the button?
Start the Big Bang in reverse
Did someone mention Dutton ..?

Learning how to bob and weave

A glaring aspect of the inquiry into the Victorian Government's response to COVAID-19 was how no one wanted to own up to the botched plan of security guards working at the quarantine hotels.
Broadcast September 25, 2020.

Hello, welcome to Lecture Theatre 3
You're smart to sign up for this course
Whether a director, manager or secretary
In health, or Government, or the force

At EVADER we are supremely skilled
Teaching tricks of public service denial
And we don't mean, 'That's the first I've heard of this!'
Or, 'It's somewhere here in the pile …'

With this invasive inquiry going on
Haranguing, questioning, and sniping
No longer can you blame a balls-up
On that nice little Greek girl in Typing

Now, EVADER stands for:

'Educating Victorian Administrators
On how to Deny Executive Responsibility'
Once you pass, you'll protect your post
No matter how modest your ability

First, it's a Diploma in Evasiveness
So they can't get a bead on you at all
Then, on to a Bachelor of Persuasiveness
Where you make a big problem sound rather small

Then up for your Masters in Mis-Communication
Where you outline how the solution was dashed
When you discovered your e-mail inbox was full
Which made the NBN crash

And not only that, your phone went flat
And your iPad fell behind the sofa
And your laptop was stolen by a homeless junkie
And you left your Fitbit at early-morning yoga

From that they'll deduce you're spiritual
But a clumsy techno oddball
So, we provide you with a Doctorate of Philosophy
Based on the thesis, 'I cannot recall'

That's the ultimate get-out statement
You'll have them running, screaming down the hall
Just stay calm and repeat it again and again
And slow proceedings down to a crawl

Your PhD also shows how to tell the court
What you claim is the project's real history
But looking at the transcripts later they'll find
A puzzle shrouded in a riddle, cloaked in a mystery

So, let's get cracking, everyone
Time to become a skilled inquiry dissuader
If you want to keep your high-paying job
We'll make you safe, that's our role at EVADER

Obsession with the 'A' Club

The US, having been the first to develop, and so far the only one to use, the atomic bomb, looks sneeringly down on anyone who dares to build one. Broadcast June 21, 2019.

Once upon a time
Not a good time
The US said, 'We love apple pie and Mom

'And only for us
'The rest, you get stuffed
'We've made this device called The Bomb'

A nasty invention
Breaking all convention
It could flatten a whole city in a blink

And in the big war
They brought it to the fore
And said, 'So, everyone, what do you think?

'Envy you must feel
'But now here's the deal
'Having shown you that mighty conflagration

'We'll run the club
'Just a few ticket stubs
'For those desiring to be a nuclear nation'

It was a poncy mob
All A-bomb snobs
Russia and Britain first at the dance

CHARDONNAY SOCIALIST *And Other Radio Poems*

And after the Chinese
Built one with ease
The Pacific was blown up by France

So, India and Pakistan
And North Korea to a man
Said, 'Well, we think we'll join the trail'

And, there might be just one other
Hiding under cover
Somewhere in the backblocks of Israel

Then along came Iran
Who said, 'Hey man,
'We love the notion of nuclear fission'

America said, 'Nay
'Give that idea away
'We're not giving you mongrels permission'

It turned into a blue
As nasty remarks flew
And the US just kept rattling the cage

But, these guys are Persian
They don't need much urging
Look at history, they're very good at rage

Now, we're all doomed
To nuclear winter gloom
If the US attacks them, all deranged

Never mind, guys
Look on the bright side
No need to worry about climate change …

After-dark questions fit for a Queen

Police quickly nabbed a young man who got into the grounds of Buckingham Palace. But had he made it to the royal boudoir, what was he going to ask the Queen?
Broadcast July 12, 2019.

Oh, here I am
Locked in the slam
In the Tower of London, being treated so mean

I think it's unfair
Being lashed to a chair
All I wanted was to have a chat with the Queen

I did it without malice
Got into the Palace
Tried to reach the royal corridors

I was like Arthur Daly
A latter day Disraeli
Seeking good counsel from 'Her Indoors'

First, I wanted to ask
Straight to the task
Don't think I'm some political amateur

I wanted her view
On why he shot through
Her former Washington Ambassador

Oh, that must grate
Those damn United States
Was she going to give the Yanks the bump?

CHARDONNAY SOCIALIST *And Other Radio Poems*

Or not let it faze her
Stay a good neighbour
And put it down to the antics of Trump?

And speaking of crazies
Barking with rabies
Emerging from this 'new world' forest

Was she remaining calm?
Or considering self-harm?
With the impending leadership of Boris

I'd ask her about Phil
Has he lost his will
Since he went and rolled the Land Rover?

And about Princess Di
The saint held so high
Does she think it will ever blow over?

Then there's a new baby
Called Archie, milady
My God, what will they think of next?

It's sorta, kinda royal
So will she stay loyal?
Or take a few zeros off the gift cheque?

But here's the big probe
Into the ermine robe
It gives poor old Charles the 'schmitz'

Please tell him M'arm
He means you no harm
But are you ever going to call it quits ..?

An idea, Your Majesty, from Sir John

Australian authorities finally released the letters from then Governor-General Sir John Kerr to Buckingham Palace in the lead-up to his 1975 dismissal of the Whitlam Government.
In a scoop, 'Friday Magazine' unearthed a letter written very late in the piece - and apparently very late at night - but which did not catch the next day's mail.
Broadcast July 17, 2020.

My dearest, glorious Majesty

It's time to come true
About why I write to you
Telling tales of what's happening to our nation

Some things have gone wrong
As Gough has come on so strong
With his plans to change us for generations

The Opposition's been tough
Knowing how to play rough
Destroying anything that displays ingenuity

And many of Gough's ministers
Are such practiced un-deliverers
They couldn't organize a piss-up in a brewery

But, I don't really care
How he keeps it all in the air
That's not why my letters drip with malice

CHARDONNAY SOCIALIST *And Other Radio Poems*

I swear by the Crown
I just want to bring him down
Because, I have to admit it, I am jealous

See, we both started equals
As two ambitious legals
With a thirst for success hard to quench

But what really stunned me
He ended up running the country
While I finished on a State Judge's bench

Not even a Federal one
Just a low-rent second one
And although it had some sort of status

While Gough held the plans
Of the nation in his hands
I was farting around with old cases

So, when he offered this post
I thought, Great Caesar's ghost
I'll be right there at the centre of the action

I'll offer Cabinet advice
With instructions precise
On ideas to provide the nation with traction

In fact, it's a toothless position
An inglorious commission
Far removed from the corridors of power

What a waste of my time
And my brilliant mind
Opening bridges and buildings and towers

Still …

There are 'reserve powers' there
Let those words hang in the air
I'm the top boss, that's my firm belief

Gough will soon see
I'm not only the G-G
I am also the Commander-in-Chief

Time to give him the boot
It'll be such a hoot
Raise the flag, whoop-whoop, ship-ahoy

Charles can take my job
And while he plays the snob
I'll run Australia as its first Vice-Roy

So there you have it
Please firmly grab it
It'll be better for all down the track

A new era is dawning
I'll get this typed up in the morning
Where's that bottle? One more nip, then the sack …

CHARDONNAY SOCIALIST   *And Other Radio Poems*

Heading north to save the day

As they say, it's impossible to predict unintended consequences. This certainly hit home when it was declared that the annual bash for Year 12 students to finish off their school years in style was another victim of COVAID-19.
Broadcast September 4, 2020.

He had lost his bronze tan
The Gold Coast tourist man
And his voice was trembling
With unbridled fear

'We'll all hit the skids
'Now those southern school kids
'Ain't gonna have their party
'Up here this year!'

He said he couldn't go on
That the lockdown was wrong
And it was unfair
To put a ban on Schoolies

So, I've devised a plan
To help him out of his jam
I'm heading north
With my group, The Old Foolies

We will be, without fail
At the other end of the scale
In this group, no one will be
Aged under seventy

So, we'll need a full-time nurse
And our own private hearse
A defibrillator in each room
An absolute necessity

And grab-handles on the showers
But, please, no flowers
'Cos the pollen will have us
Up all night sneezing

In turn, cylinders of oxygen
And oodles of amoxicillin
To stop the flu, the coughing
And the wheezing

Comfy beds for old backs
And door hooks to hang slacks
Are a must, of course, for
This aging adventure

And can we stay near a Coles?
That stocks Dr Scholl's?
And Polident on special
For our dentures?

But don't worry about us
There'll be no noise and fuss
We have our games
And some of them are corkers

CHARDONNAY SOCIALIST *And Other Radio Poems*

Books for colouring in
Making picture frames out of tin
And seeing who can stand longest
Without his or her walker

Oh, I know we're in lockdown
And the borders are in block down
But you can trust us
We're clever old commuters

We'll go north by the back roads
And emerge from the shadows
A mighty herd
Of mobility scooters

So just be patient
Don't be a complainant
Once we reach the 'Goldie'
We'll ease the fiscal tension

Our Old Foolies revival
Will lead to your survival
As we go nuts
After we collect our pensions …

The beginning of the end for Facebook?

The link between Facebook, Donald Trump, his 2016 election, and a geeky research company had many people alarmed over the issue of personal data being harvested. Not the least being Mark Zuckerberg. Broadcast March 23, 2017.

Is this the end of Facebook?
The family and friends chase book?
It's a classic investors case-book
Of a share price starting to wobble

This social media ace book
The 'just touching base' book
And runaway blistering pace book
Is stuck in a political squabble

Those tech-heads in disgrace book
How did they use up Facebook?
And turn it into a debased book
Shaking its founder to the core?

The shares are up for the dump
'Cos they made some data jump
Ensuring voters put in Trump
And shoved Hillary out the door

CHARDONNAY SOCIALIST — *And Other Radio Poems*

Zuckerberg's joined the fray
Because he's made lots of hay
Up and down Wall Street way
A link he does not want to sever

But his fears are rapidly growing
There are others issues flowing
The sign-ups have been slowing
With many logging off forever

So, who's leaving Facebook?
The friends and family chase book?
Who's exiting the touching-base book?
It's Gen Z that is jumping ship

Seeking a new social space nook
They're pulling out of Facebook
Saying it's no longer an ace look
When your Nanna thinks it's hip …

Clap, clap, it's the ScoMo Rap

Having emerged from the Coalition leadership coup that made him the accidental Prime Minister, I figured a marketing man like Scott Morrison would go straight into the recording studio and lay down a track to set the template for his new role.
September 21, 2018.

I'm your average guy
A bloke from next door
At a niece's wedding
I'm on the dance floor
Being hip and gnarly
And bustin' my moves
It's a treat to watch
My middle-aged grooves

A Cronulla Man
I go down town
To a footy pie night
And get around
In my rugby jersey
And my baseball cap
Don't wanna be seen
In a John Howard hat
That's old fashioned
And just a little bit musty
Sort of like singin'
The Best of Slim Dusty

CHARDONNAY SOCIALIST *And Other Radio Poems*

'Cos I'm the coolest leader
Since Malcolm Fraser
I'm the Big Show now
Not the curtain raiser
I know how to do
The hip and the hop
While singing out loud
From the hill top
And wearing the bling
And shaking mah booty
To the latest hit,
'Oh, Tutti Frutti …'

It was the right thing
To oust the PM
He was past his prime
Going 'round the bend
Hiding down his hole
Like a nasty pit viper
Did he see it comin'?
Not from Point Piper

'Tho I must admit
It was news to me
I didn't know about it
Until I saw the ABC

Right from the start
I jumped the gun
With the aged care row
I hit a home run
Those poor old folks
With the wispy hair
Sitting in the dark
Gasping for air

No need for insiders
No need for informers
I set things up
Before Four Corners
As for Liberal voters
I'm no fool
I dished out the money
To every private school

See ...
I'm right up with it
I'm walking real tall
I'm a shape-shifter
With a crystal ball

You can see how it goes
When I enter the House
They step back and say
'Man, that dude's grouse ...'

CHARDONNAY SOCIALIST — *And Other Radio Poems*

PNG takes them all for a ride

To show they were worthy of the big league, when it hosted APEC, Papua New Guinea chauffeured its world leader guests around in a somewhat unique style.
Broadcast November 23, 2018.

It was in Moresby they all met up
In their finest island get-up
The show-offs, the crazies, the foolhardy

They couldn't wait to get to town
To be driven round and round
In, of all things, a brand new Maserati

Why leader Peter O'Neil
Chose to spin the wheels
Of such a set of costly cars remains a mystery

For the place is hardly wealthy
The Treasury's not too healthy
In a country rooted in deepest, darkest history

Dear old Mahathir did arrive
As did the Sultan of Brunei
To APEC, a kinda Pacific political Tinder

There was Abe and Trudeau
And Joko Widodo
And nothing could stop the smile of Jacinda

Peru and Mexico
Sent their guys to the show
With Hong Kong and the others to sit and clap

Not forgetting of course
The strangest dark horse
The Daggy Aussie in his various baseball caps

But where was mighty Putin?
The idol of shootin' and tootin'?
Why did he give this summit the dump?

Was it because the other big ace
Was not showing his face
The man who thinks he's President, Donald Trump

They both made the mistake
Of sending the second mate
Leaving the stage to the big man from China

Xi Jinping was in tough mode
Promulgating Belt and Road
And causing much political angina

So the VP from the States
Called on his Aussie mates
And said, 'I have a mighty plan

'We'll build an air force base
'Spread guns all over this place
'Then I'm off to carpet-bomb Iran'

ScoMo became enlightened
His face began to brighten
'I'm with you, let's build some mighty towers

CHARDONNAY SOCIALIST *And Other Radio Poems*

'And run cables everywhere
'Along the ground and in the air
'And give this nation some fair dinkum power'

Not that far down the road
Amid another overload
His constituents felt as if they'd been cursed

'Hey, boss,' they cried in pain
'The grid's under strain again
'How about giving *us* some decent power first ..?'

The leaders then flew home
Having chewed the best of the bone
Without so much as a final communiqué

Leaving angry cops to pillaging
Rather than sitting happily villaging
And heading the country into total disarray

Appeals are rarely appealing

Yet another negative result, for a refugee who challenged a Border Security ruling, raised the question: Are legal appeals ever worth it? Broadcast September 14, 2018.

As an Appeals Court Judge
I try not to begrudge
People before me seeking an act of contrition

As their last-chance trial
They hope I'll reconcile
And change my learned brother's earlier decision

So I hold all the clout
That's what its about
When they're on their knees seeking a new probe

From this poncy old prig
Sporting a horse-hair wig
Lunette glasses and a flouncy ermine robe

I love their earnest faces
As they play all their aces
In the belief that they have something new

I sift through the traces
Of the paper-thin basis
On which they are hoping a reversal is due

CHARDONNAY SOCIALIST *And Other Radio Poems*

What they don't understand
Is the law of the land
And the concept of a system of diversity

They come undermanned
Like a leaderless band
A shame they never went to university

See, I studied at Oxford
Where my intellect prospered
Under ancient dons teaching Law of Tort

With the odd mark doctored
I was lovingly fostered
To defend the barriers of the legal fort

So, you sad little man
What's that in your hand?
A file you've prepared with hope and passion?

You must understand
Whatever you've planned
It won't be read, unless it's writ in Latin

Stop that derision!
Here's my decision
You've tried to show the judgement was vexed

But your view is askew
You gave nothing new
A load of gravel. Where's my gavel? Appeal dismissed. Who's next?

A cold, black heart on display

Scott Morrison had only been Prime Minister for a few months when a Bill was introduced to allow the medical transfer of ill asylum seekers from Nauru to the mainland for treatment. Would the Government show some compassion and pass this before the House broke up for Christmas?
Broadcast December 7, 2018.

And so there they sat
Shouting this and barking that
A load of insults, hot air and bluster

In the House of Parlay
Our leaders on display
Mounting a classic filibuster

The idea of this is
Get your opponents in a tizz
By dragging debate on forever

Hoping the subject of the fray
Will simply go away
Leaving the vote in the Never Never

At the centre of it all
Looming large and tall
Bumptious, wild-eyed and mouthy

Was our PM from hell
At top decibels
The Right Honourable Mr Pouty Shouty

CHARDONNAY SOCIALIST — *And Other Radio Poems*

Subtlety's not for him
With that supercilious grin
And a manner haughty and overbearing

When they gave out characteristics
He took the box marked 'ballistics'
And by-passed 'caring' and 'sharing'

Oh, pass me the gin
How we ended up with him
Is a query not even he can answer

He shut the House down
Put on the dressing gown
While the inertia spread like a cancer

Played it hard and dirty
Closed it at four-thirty
Said Merry Christmas and then shot through

Using brutal tactics
And clever didactics
Avoiding the vote on the sick kids of Nauru

Was there a better sample
A more egregious example
Of a leader with no moral compass?

Sailing in cross-factional circles
At a rate of knots he hurtles
Across the dark seas of social injustice

Catching up with old what's-his-name

After Papua New Guinea cozied up to China at the APEC meeting, Prime Minister Morrison figured it might be a good idea for Australia to say hello to its Pacific neighbours. Whoever they were …
Broadcast January 18, 2019.

I'm taking leave from the House
Feeling it would be so creative
To fly over the Pacific Ocean
And say hello to the natives

Time for an Oz leader to land
On the shores of Fiji blue
Then I'll get in my bus, er, plane
And visit Vanuatu, too

I think that's where I'm going
Don't shame me with blame
These islands, to a Cronulla boy
Look all the bloody same

Yes, my critics will declare
I've got political angina
From all the cash being spent over here
By those wily bastards from China

I say the locals are doing it tough
In the backblocks of the Pacific
They've got a lot to worry about
Tho' don't ask me to be specific

CHARDONNAY SOCIALIST *And Other Radio Poems*

We just want to show these folk
We're taking their plight seriously
So, first we grab a stack of cash
And throw it around deliriously

The next decision in the plan
Is to make the place look swank
It's a typical, sneaky Western ploy
To set up an infrastructure bank

That's generally the way to do it
Been no better method yet
Build and build and build some more
And saddle them with the debt

The next item in the story
Is a military matter, of course
Building camps, bases and airstrips
And a Defence Training Force

To keep things under control
We must have our people all day
Pulling the locals into line
And being masters of all we survey

So we'll need more diplomats
Ah, jobs for my lawyer mates
A gin at sunset on the veranda
All at the best of mates rates

It's the classic white man's way
Of keeping things bright and sunny
Peacefully taking over the Pacific
With guns, lawyers and money

Here's your visa, ma Cherie

Arrest, jail, and/or expulsion are the main risks for refugees. But if you are a French au pair, apparently that's a different matter. Broadcast September 7, 2018.

The immovable Peter Dutton
Pushed the big button
And invoked his famous stare

With a stroke of his pen
He let her in again
This deserving French au pair

What else could he do?
Make her shoot through?
That'd be a bit on the nose

Said Gillon McLachlan
'She'll work for my cousin
'And then play for the Adelaide Crows'

And, the other rapscallion?
The curvaceous Italian?
She, too, got 'em all in her thrall

'Oh, let's not be petty
'She'll cook great spaghetti
'For the Secret Policeman's Ball'

CHARDONNAY SOCIALIST *And Other Radio Poems*

That's how it's done
Under the Great Southern sun
If you want to stay on our shores

Just be in the know
And it's all systems go
Or 'Back on your boat, here's your oars!'

Black holes and other devices

The year 2019 saw an early Budget brought on by the Treasurer because an election was looming.
Broadcast April 5, 2019.

It's fun to be the Treasurer
The economic measurer
Of the nation's fiscal standing and its economic status

Whether it's making dough
Or travelling somewhat slow
Or in that nether, neutral state of financial hiatus

Whatever the reality
There's a historic duality
You must trot out to shore up your position

First, you warmly state
The future's looking great
And in good hands 'cos of your brilliant vision

Then, you must declare
Something bad is in the air
And you're concerned by words of your forecasters

Then, point to the other side
With a look that's, oh, so snide
And blame everything on those previous bastards

No matter how time's gone by
Adopt the ground that's high
And say you inherited a financial 'black hole'

CHARDONNAY SOCIALIST   *And Other Radio Poems*

This is your number one excuse
So you can dish out more abuse
About all those lazy bludgers on the dole

Bad roads, no tracks, slow trains
Rave on about the pain
Inflicted on us all by your predecessors

No work, no pay, no jobs
Everyone's a lazy slob
Say it's a challenge to clean up all the messes

Add it's a tough world out there
But you're trying to make it fair
Say you know ordinary folk will get the picture

Take a few bucks off their power
Offer a tax cut worth an hour
While you quietly make the rich folk even richer

That's the name of the game
Slot your opponents in the frame
And dish up smoke, mirrors and deflection

Say it's best for our nation
A sort of fiscal aeration
And nothing to do with the upcoming election …

Travels with Smiley ScoMo and Baleful Bill

At last, time for the big test at the polls. Initially the 2019 election was as dull as dishwater, but then the two main head-butters started zipping all over the nation and things fired up.
Broadcast May 3, 2019.

On the plane
Off the plane
Around they go once more

On the bus
Off the bus
Come knocking at your door

They're scouring the entire nation
All aboard for a polling thrill
With wily Smiley ScoMo
And battling Baleful Bill

Smiley's got his V8 revving
He's playing the underdog
The good old Aussie battler
Sittin' on the campfire log

CHARDONNAY SOCIALIST   *And Other Radio Poems*

And talking up the nation
In a voice upbeat and brash
And eatin' pies and scoffin' snags
And givin' the grog a lash

Down at the shearing shed
He gets grease on his strides
Pulling a lamb through the hatch
Giving it a short back and sides

He works the country halls
Plays footy, tennis and soccer
Shirt-sleeves at the barbecue
'How are they danglin', Ocker?'

Sports a winner's look
Bares teeth with a sparkling glow
Gives the distinct impression
He knows he's in with a show

'Cos Baleful Bill is so straight
The epitome of Mr Cool
Looking so sure he'll be
Head Boy of Canberra School

He wears a suit, sports a tie
And amid the dust and flies
Is very circumspect about
The way he eats his pies

Trying to look in control
And not putting one foot wrong
Keeping everything under wraps
Until they ring the final gong

But is he running a little too flat?
A bit short on pace and passion
Instead of fire, rage and colour
It's all cold and bleak and ashen

Baleful Bill better lift his game
And start giving things a shake
Otherwise he might go the way
Of John Hewson's birthday cake …

CHARDONNAY SOCIALIST *And Other Radio Poems*

When hopes and dreams go up in flames

For many buyers of tower apartments, cracks, leaks, collapses and killer fires have proved disastrous. But just who should take responsibility soon becomes a murky issue.
Broadcast July 19, 2019.

Hello there!

I'm the major developer
Of your apartment in the sky
The one you paid nine hundred thousand for
And is now worth less then five ...

Don't bother chasing me
About a unit rendered useless
I know how to set things up
So tracking me is fruitless

My business is in the Caymans
I change my spots like a leopard
The only name on the Company Board
Is Lenny, my German Shepherd

Ah, G'day.

I'm the contracted builder
I'm like the developer too
The moment things start going wrong
I'm in my Merc and shooting through

63

And while everyone is in tears
Reaching for the Kleenex
I quietly liquidate my old firm
And rise again, just like the phoenix

Ni ha!

I'm Ching Wang Chong from China
At the other end of the scale
I'm the long-suffering plasterer
Who's scared I'll go to jail

If I don't whack these walls together
And stay as quiet as the sphinx of Giza
They'll take the rest of my miserable pay
And tear up my dodgy visa

Good afternoon.

I'm the project architect
But don't paint me as a conspirator
The plans looked fine when they left my office
Anything else, talk to my solicitor!

How the heck are ya?

I'm everyone's mate, the carpenter
You can call me 'Nails'
But I'm not the chippy in charge
See, it's all a matter of scale

I was appointed by someone
Much further up the line
To build this mighty manor
In a lunatic amount of time

CHARDONNAY SOCIALIST   *And Other Radio Poems*

And over there's the plumber
And that's his best mate, 'Sparks'
They've been bullied into this
By a pair of financial sharks

They'll have to fight for their cash
It's a customary industry pain
No wonder you get electric shocks
And blockages in your drains

Welcome to the Press Conference

See this serious look on my face?
I'm the suitably angry Minister
I don't want the State to pay for this
I'll chase those acting sinister

When it comes to spotting the guilty
There's no one braver and bolder
Oh, I'm afraid we must call this off
It seems I'm a major shareholder …

To the Premier

I'm the building inspector
I creep quietly onto the site
A ghostly, anxious spectre
Hoping everything's all right

But if things go belly-up
Please don't go blaming me
I can only give my okay
To what the builder lets me see

I used to work for the Council
And they were so much tougher
Now, I can't insure my own business
Oh, please don't make me suffer!

To the import agent

Our workers are proud of their products
In our new business park in China
When it comes to buying our cladding
You couldn't have imported anything finer

Sure, it might be flammable
But the flames are warm and hearty
And if you've got any more complaints
Take 'em up with the Communist Party

Hello, everyone

I'm an engineering consultant
I predicted this project would fail
Can I suggest some ways to fix it up?
After you've taken my bank details …

Arrghh!!

You described this place as Nirvana
When off the plan I bought it
Now you bastards have gone to ground
And no one wants to sort it

The place is totally worthless
Full of cracks and leaks and stench
And I spend my nights under three raincoats
Huddled on a cold park bench

CHARDONNAY SOCIALIST *And Other Radio Poems*

Um, is there anyone out there?

I'm the poor old taxpayer
Now stuck with this bill of excess
And left to wonder once again
How did we get into such a mess ..?

How the unlosable was lost

Even the bookies had paid out on the ALP before the May 2019 poll. But in politics, as in sport, not everything goes as planned. And it certainly didn't for ALP leader Bill Shorten.
Broadcast May 24, 2019.

What the #&*% happened, Bill?
Do you feel a bit of a dill?
You climbed the highest mountain
And ended up over the hill

What went wrong? What turned sour?
Why did voters give you the boot?
Perhaps one thing that hurt you badly
Was always wearing that suit

Looked snappy, but far too dark
A sombre and ghostly spectre
You gave the impression of wanting to be
A full-time funeral director

Whereas ScoMo rolled his sleeves up
And got in amongst the crowd
Swinging bats and throwing balls
And telling his story out loud

It wasn't much of a story
In close-up, it was rather thin
But he told it and told it and told it some more
Slowly drawing the voters in

CHARDONNAY SOCIALIST *And Other Radio Poems*

Meanwhile, you talked about money
You talked about taxes and banking
You threatened retired old geezers
They'd lose their much-loved franking

They then phoned up the talk-back
And related in shuddering fright
How they'd cry about losing their dough
And couldn't sleep at all at night

That affected their children
Who turned right against you
'Cos they not only feared for Mum and Dad
But their Last Will and Testament too …

You continued your aggression
Attacking the Top End of Town
What about the Top End of the Nation?
That also brought you down

Queensland's a separate world
They do it their own way up there
They dig big holes, and sell trucks of coal
And say, 'Bugger the state of the air!'

You should have listened to the Q&A man
Who said you'd kick an own goal
That you'd lose the unlosable election
That you'd defy the bookies and polls

What will really hurt, what will really gall
In this world that so brutally condemns
You and John Hewson will never get a bed
In the 'Rest Home for Ex-PMs'

Party for some, agony for others

If you want to know where most of the world's troubles began, you don't have to look far. As the new US Embassy was being opened in Jerusalem, not that far away, blood was being spilt.
Broadcast May 18, 2018.

Drones buzzing, tear gas flying
Children running, mothers crying
Hell comes to earth
In a modern day war
Bearing the hallmarks
Of ancient times before

Guns firing, tanks rumbling
Angry young men stumbling
Across rocky ground
In the firing zone
Their only weapon
A sling-shot and stone

Tyres burning, smoke rising
Drilled soldiers are mobilizing
To end it all now
Let's put it to bed
Bang. Bang. Bang.
And sixty are dead

An hour's drive away
Far from the affray
The images are mesmerizing
Smirking leaders socializing

CHARDONNAY SOCIALIST *And Other Radio Poems*

Opening a building
Dressed to the nines
Glad-handing big-shot friends
And sprouting familiar lines

This is our land, not our fault
We would love to bring it to a halt
But they won't listen
They are not understanding
It's our heaven-sent right
To keep on expanding

Of course we want peace
A two state solution
But we'll keep the guns loaded
To stall revolution

But maybe this time, the moralizing
Simply won't work, it's so polarizing

Incidents like this
Can resonate for years
Amid the blood and the dust and the tears
Could this be the beginning of the end
The Achilles heel
Of a leadership that refuses to yield

Time for a change
Time to draw back the clouds and let in the sun
Time to end the rule of the tank and the gun

In a modern day war
With all the baggage
Of times before
There comes a day when the trumpet calls
And lo and behold, the giant falls

All in our own drone zone

The drone is a fun toy for kids, can be very productive in industry, and is a brilliant device for taking photographs. But the military application is another thing.
Broadcast June 29, 2018.

I'm sitting quietly on my own
Flying my nifty drone
And having a rather enjoyable day

Why, the sky, it's so blue
There's a colourful rainbow, too
And the cows are gently mooing away

But I have to confess
In my pursuit of success
On a mission so important and profound

I'm staring at my monitor
And checking its speedometer
In a bunker twenty metres under ground

See, it's actually a spy craft
From sharp nose to sleek aft
Its shape best described as reptilian

It streaks through the air
With guile and speed and flair
And in dollars, cost only a mere billion

CHARDONNAY SOCIALIST *And Other Radio Poems*

Oh, I'm so tough and brave
Down in my military cave
Guiding the drone's course by degrees

For my Government's vision
And our number one mission
Is to spy on those wily old Chinese

It's our job to bust 'em
'Cos you just can't trust 'em
So we're taking footage of what we can see

How dare they work so hard
To build a new back yard
In a place called the South China Sea

Hey, China, shoot through!
That's not exclusively for you!
Your expansion there positively reeks

We have as much right
To sail through day and night
'Tho to get there, it takes us three weeks …

Someone's got inside my fridge

One day Prime Minister Scott Morrison very solemnly declared that we should be exceedingly concerned because someone was doing, um, something to, er, someone else ...
Broadcast June 26, 2020.

I listen to every word the PM says
Believing all that he states is true
For example last week he seriously said
Someone's been hacking us out of the blue

He mentioned Lion and BlueScope and Toll
But the one that made me feel unwell
Was he said they've got inside the computer
Of the famous Fisher & Paykel

And I know that that is for certain
I can tell you it's ridgy-didge
'Cos since ScoMo made his announcement
I swear something's wrong with me fridge

Those dastardly hacker attackers
They've turned everything upside down
One minute my butter has melted
And my celery is turning dark brown

And then the next, the milk's gone cold again
And the yoghurt is frozen too
And if I poke my head inside for three seconds
My ears turn a distinct shade of blue

CHARDONNAY SOCIALIST — *And Other Radio Poems*

By gee, they're insidious, these hackers
Defying all laws of physics
Making temperature changes within seconds
In a reverse-cycle white goods gimmick

I suppose it could be worse
I could have a disturbed dishwasher too
Or perhaps a wanderlust washing machine
With a deranged dryer to boot

Wait, hang on, look at this!
I've found the cause of misuse
See, when I was vacuuming
I kicked the fridge power-plug loose

What a terrible thing to do to a bloke
Filling my mind with thoughts unclear
ScoMo and his cryptic warnings
Are designed purely to fill us with fear

He's so circumspect with what he says
Ultra coy about who's behind all this
Scarily saying it is all high security
But not declaring who it actually is

Well, let me throw this into the mix
Turning things round, if you please
Did you know that since 2012
Fisher & Paykel has been owned by the Chinese ..?

It began with the Three 'Wise' Men

It was a horrible moment that left us all hollow. The New Zealand mosque slaughter. Where did all this begin? For me, there is a simple answer.
Broadcast March 22, 2019.

The door is swung open
To 'Welcome, brother'
But standing on the step
Is a guest like no other

A devil from the darkness
A spectre out of hell
Spewing bullets and hatred
From the same shell

Black gun glistening
Masked in childish scrawl
Scratching old sores
'Kill invaders' is the call

With spite and loathing
And venom and hate
Watches the bodies fall
Two, four, six, eight

No man, nor woman
Nor child can hide
From a merciless killer
On an evil joyride

CHARDONNAY SOCIALIST *And Other Radio Poems*

How can any heart
Be turned so black?
As to embark on such
A merciless attack?

It's the end result
Of an insidious narrative
Pointing to differences
Making the comparative

Painting others as evil
Threatening and dangerous
Saying they stand for one thing
To slowly endanger us

So who is to blame?
Who got us into this mess?
It started with a drum-beat
The beating of the chest

The Three 'Wise' Men
Invaded a sovereign nation
Expecting to find WMDs
And victory and adoration

But they got it all wrong
And after two decades
This is the awful fallout
That haunts us in spades

Doesn't worry the trio
As around the world they flash
Flogging their heroic tales
For a bucket load of cash

That's very small comfort
To a quake-shattered town
That was just getting up
Only to be again struck down

CHARDONNAY SOCIALIST — *And Other Radio Poems*

Swim for freedom

When Melbourne was put into Lockdown 2, every other state did not want to have a bar of us Victorians and shut us out. What to do if you want to get out of the place?
Broadcast July 10, 2020.

Ssshhh, quiet!

I'm escaping from Victoria
Evading Dan's lockdown order
I'm way up here, with my gear
On the New South Wales border

And the heart of my plan
Sets my taste buds all aquiver
I've heard the town of Corowa
Has the best pizza on the river!

There's D'Amico's Italian
Where I could try the Portofino
With king prawns and mozzarella
And a bottle of house vino

Or I could go to Ricky D's
And have the Calabrese
All hot salami and tomato
And said to be very, very cheesy

I did this menu research
About my dietary needs
'Cos once I've swum the river
I'll need a nice, reviving feed

Oh, right, didn't I tell you?
No attempt by car for me
I'm diving in the Murray River
And swimming like buggery

In the middle of the night
When no-one's around
In a wetsuit plus a bag of clothes
For when I make ground

And if I can't cross at Corowa
There's lots of accessible towns
Like Mulwala, or Tocumwal
Or possibly Murray Downs

Or Moama or Buronga
Or Barham or Barooga
Or Howlong or Tooleybuc
Or good old Cobramunga

And after I come ashore
I won't wander back and forth
I aim to keep on going
To the deepest, farthest North

To the very top of Oz
Where it's nice and hot and sticky
Although getting into Queensland
Could be a little tricky

But I'm sure I'll convince them
To let me go on my way
If I finish every sentence
With a long drawn out, 'Heyyyy…?'

CHARDONNAY SOCIALIST *And Other Radio Poems*

So this is goodbye, Dan
Too late for your ideas conciliar
It all blew up when your hotel guards
Got a fraction over-familiar

Now everyone is imprisoned
To the harshest of degrees
With people at their tower windows
Staring longingly at the trees

Oooh, wait, before I jump
I've just had a thought
Would it be really all that clever
To escape the Andrews Fort?

What if I'm arrested
And classed as a refugee?
And Peter Dutton declares
He'll take 'special' care of me?

And re-opens Manus Island
Just for my accommodation
As a clear and present warning
To the remainder of the nation?

Hmmm, well, before I jump
Into the cold Murray drink
I'll sit down, have a smoke
And another little think …

Heavy is the knock at the door

Increasing restrictions on the media came to a head when the Australian Federal Police raided the headquarters of the ABC and the home of journalist Annika Smethurst.
Broadcast June 7, 2019.

Good morning, Madam

I'm a federal copper
A red-cheeked, thick-neck whopper
And you can't stop me marching right through your front door

To look around your place
With a stony, gormless face
And do some heavy breathing as I rifle through your drawers ...

We don't seek a cheap thrill
A stash of pot, or night-club pill
Although that might help us with our accusations

We have a higher aim
To apportion you the blame
Of stealing documents to imperil our mighty nation

You've been a naughty girl
You make my toes curl
Have you no respect for the concept of Sovereign Borders?

After we've given you a fright
And told you what to write
We'll knock on the door of those bastards at 'Four Corners'

CHARDONNAY SOCIALIST *And Other Radio Poems*

We know the grand aim
Is to send our nation up in flames
You evil reporters, and broadcasters, and columnists

If Menzies'd had his way
None of you'd be free today
You'd be breaking rocks, you card-carrying Communists

Don't tie this in with Dutton
He'll say he knows nuttin'
Stating calmly this is not within his environs

And leave the PM alone
Right now he's before the Throne
The Queen thinks he's the chief of the Solomon Islands

Let me tell you a little secret
Can I trust you? Can you keep it?
The timing of this was to create a different complexion

We had planned all of this
Plus the arrival of the Chinese ships
To embarrass Labor, but they went and lost the election!

Well, we're nearly done
It has been so much fun
After this, I doubt you'll push your luck so far

I'll only be a jiffy
Just taking some evidence with me
Into the bag, this frilly-laced, purple, wonder bra …

Ice melt is serious business

Come the end of the year, the end of a decade. Should be a celebration. But as Santa reflects on his latest trip around the world, things are looking dark for the future.
Broadcast December 27, 2019.

I wonder what Santa thinks
Now he's done the Christmas run
And got home to find that more ice
Has been melted by the sun

And his North Pole base is drifting
As the temperature steadily rises
They reckon by 2051
It'll be off the coast of Hawaii

His cheeks are red 'cos he's angry
His nose is vermillion with rage
He's mad at us for doing so little
About ongoing climate change

His family is breaking up
He hasn't seen Mrs Claus in ages
She's lost thirty kilos and had plastic done
And is serving cocktails in Las Vegas

Then there's Rudolph, Comet and Cupid
And Dasher, Dancer and Chancer
And Vixen, Blixem and Dunder
And that poncy smart-arse named Prancer

CHARDONNAY SOCIALIST *And Other Radio Poems*

They're fulfilling a long-held dream
Pulling an extraordinary switch
Touring the world as a tribute band
To Dave Dee, Dozy, Beaky, Mick and Titch

And don't go near the upset elves
That once merry little group
Is furious that the Arctic Ocean
Is now as warm as chicken soup

They've gone across to the other side
Via a devious flow and ebb
Shutting the workshop and selling the toys
On the deepest darkest web

So, Santa won't turn up next year
Unless the ice-melt stops
He'll be on a Li-Lo drinking beer
Bingeing Netflix in his jocks

The highs and highs of being a stockbroker

Many years ago I wrote that the stock market was little more than a lottery for spoilt, private-schooled screen jockeys. Little has changed. Broadcast October 12, 2018.

I'm a stockbroker
A top market stoker
Making shares go ballistic and rocket up or down

It's an insular profession
All about possession
Making money for myself and the big end of town

We just shout 'Sell'
Ignite the bombshell
And orchestrate a crash in the blink of an eye

Then, when no-one's looking
We re-set all the bookings
And before you know it, baby, we're reached another high

Flying up on our own
A greedy fiscal drone
Our over-view on life is nothing less than ruthless

'Cos there's no alarm
If a client drops the farm
Any control over us is completely bloody toothless

CHARDONNAY SOCIALIST *And Other Radio Poems*

It's all about the self
Grab the money off the shelf
While twisting and turning and bending every rule

No need to get fraught
If you do get caught
The judge up there will have gone to your old school

See, we dropped the ball
Sparking the GFC fall
People lost their jobs and a lot of companies failed

But we shifted the blame
Manipulated the game
We might have been the cause but none of us was jailed

So, it's a great to be a broker
Not for us the mediocre
Living the flashy lifestyle high up on the hog

Buying jewellery and cars
Drinking at trendy bars
And swapping information on the early morning jog

Living in a fiscal bubble
A sort of Wall Street hubble
We come and go, high and low, on a monetary trip

That will never end
Lots of cash round the bend
Before I head off skiing, can I give you the latest tip ..?

Duty to the shareholder

In the last 30 years, the insatiable greed of the 'haves' has caused enormous social damage. This can all be traced back to when a particular phrase became the mantra.
Broadcast February 22, 2019.

It's the phrase that appeals
To those that make deals
Making them go harder and bolder

While down on the floor
Amid the hard-working poor
It just makes the blood run colder

'Cos it's a major excuse
For worker abuse
For cutting, slashing and sacking

Whether in retail or wholesale
Or mining, or dining
Or media, or fashion, or fracking

See, up there on high
With the biggest cut of pie
Rustling sheafs of scrip in a folder

The board says to a man
'Let it all hit the fan
'We have our duty to the shareholder'

CHARDONNAY SOCIALIST *And Other Radio Poems*

It was never a theme
In the mainstream
Until coined by a smart-arse academic

He said it in the Eighties
And it spread like rabies
Casting wide in a fiscal pandemic

It's a top end mantra
A board-room tantra
'We have to hold everything tight'

It's in business press
Every keynote address
And on the six o'clock news at night

At annual meetings
If there's any bleating
The chair will state firm as a rock

'We're holding fast
'We're here to last
'Protecting our rich little flock'

But many now say
Must it stay this way?
Will the have-nots be left to moulder?

Or will Shorten's revolution
Bring quick retribution
And the shareholder will get the cold shoulder?

You can trust me, I'm a banker

Flash suits, even flasher cars, the word 'banker' became sullied over the years. And then the Royal Commission came to town.
Broadcast February 8, 2019.

I'm the luckiest of men
I was born to be a banker
I'm the gun full-forward
Not your average half-back flanker

I know everything about money
After which you all may hanker
But when it comes to real life
My mind could not be blanker

Still, I'm hearing what you say
Your perception growing danker
When it comes to describing me
You call me a bloody … 'canker'

That's an olde-worlde worde
It gave 'cancer' its first start
And you think I'm the tumour
Eating out your fiscal heart

Yes, I am seeing your point
As I wallow 'round in cash
Wearing bespoke suits
And driving cars oh so flash

CHARDONNAY SOCIALIST *And Other Radio Poems*

As I screw over my clients
And nail 'em to the wall
Bill 'em when they're dead
That's the best fun of it all

Changing contract terms
And holding up cash flow
From a gilded board-room
At the end of Mahogany Row

But spare a thought for me
I sleep each night alone
As my wife lies next to me
Weeping into her phone

Whispering to dearest friends
If she could, she'd make the dash
But fears how life would be
If I turn off her supply of cash

Now, 'the man' came to town
With a royal commission gun
He said, 'Pull your heads in
'This is the end of all the fun'

And that feisty girl lawyer
Made us look a nasty mob
Time was, I'd send my driver round
To offer her a job

So now we've said 'mea culpa'
And lost a few good men
But nothing will really change
We'll go back to taws again

If you don't believe me
I wouldn't smile and scoff
See what happened today
Our share price took right off

Now, I'm lunching on my yacht
Away from the cry and rancour
Having spilled my life's story
Without using the word w-w-w …

… weigh anchor, captain
And set sail for Noosa

CHARDONNAY SOCIALIST — *And Other Radio Poems*

What happened to Sam?

He was the darling of the media, and considered a future ALP star. But it all came crashing down for Sam Dastyari, the chirpy Senator from NSW.
Broadcast December 15, 2017.

What happened to Sam?
To Sam? To Dastyari Sam?
They lopped his head right off
Like a machete through a yam

How did all this happen?
Does anyone understand?
Well, Sam's main problem
Was, um, Sam being Sam …

Sam was a PR machine
With that dark wavy hair
And that ever-smiling face
And that perky Persian flair

But where he went wrong
And brought himself grief
Was eating too many plates
Of hot Mongolian beef

And after he got some bills
Paid by a Chinese bloke
The Government took a stick
And poked and poked and poked

Now, everybody knows
Both sides flash the cash
All those powerbrokers
Stump up dough in a flash

Here, take a closer look
This is all a bit of a joke
Here's a picture of the PM
With the same Chinese bloke!

What of some ex-Ministers?
Sitting high on the export perch?
Ah, s'pose you cannot blame them
After all those years of research

But just because Sam said
The mighty South China Sea
Is not the place for us
They've hit him vehemently

They claim that he's a spy
And lost his sense of reason
They want to string him up
After charging him with treason

We should really pull away
From there and other lands
Such as Syria and Iraq
And poor sad Afghanistan

No, they made Sam a target
To take the heat off them
A nasty bunch of plonkers
Full of bile and phlegm

CHARDONNAY SOCIALIST — *And Other Radio Poems*

No policies, no abilities
Nor wit, nor hint of charm
The worst Liberal Government
Since that of Billy McMahon

So, sadly, it's all over
Shock across the land
Sam can no longer claim
That he's a Senate man

But this saga really started
Many, many years ago
When his parents never once said
'No, Sam, no ..!'

Pissed off at the petrol pump

After there was a disruption of Saudi Arabian oil supply and the petrol price shot up overnight, it was too much to bear.
Broadcast September 20, 2019.

Excuse me, I have to go
I have an appointment with the bank
I've got to re-mortgage the house again
So I can fill my Corolla's tank

I'm down to my last litre
I tap the needle and pray to heaven
I can limp to my local service station
Where it's now a dollar ninety-seven

Of course they're full of excuses
They say, 'Don't start getting rowdy
'It's not us that's doing this
'It's what happened over in Saudi'

That is a deliberate get-out
Coming down from lofty towers
An incident half a world away
And the price is up within hours!

What a national disgrace
How can that possibly be?
Applying a massive hike to oil
That's still out on the sea

CHARDONNAY SOCIALIST   *And Other Radio Poems*

It's bare-faced burglary
From a bunch of profit ghouls
They know we'll buy at any price
Us needy fuel-seeking fools

Look …

We know there's a discount cycle
Running every four to six weeks
The price is up seven to eleven days
That's plenty of havoc to wreak

The other disturbing element
That hits you in the eye
Is that resources-rich Australia
Has barely two months oil supply!

We no longer refine our own
On an island surrounded by it!
Why we aren't self-sufficient
That, I just cannot buy it

So, I'm looking at an alternative
Don't wipe me off as a dreamer
Hand me that big copper kettle thing
I'm building my own Stanley Steamer …

Christopher? He's doing just Pyne

We'll miss Christopher Pyne. At his outrageous peak in his various roles in Defence, it was time closer for an examination.
Broadcast December 14, 2018.

I'm Christopher Pyne
And I'm doing just fine
Running Defence from the top

I'm holding the reins
Of shiny jet planes
At a mere hundred million a pop

And we're in a new club
Bought a French sub
Top of the range maritime

It'll hiss and splash
And costs lots of cash
We get one in eleven years' time!

It's a wonderful job
For an Adelaide snob
All about the bash and crash

Order a few tanks
And give hearty thanks
I don't have to stump up the cash

CHARDONNAY SOCIALIST — *And Other Radio Poems*

So I'm out and about
On the lookout
For a nation we can invade

I want to jump in
To a military win
And put old Monash in the shade

Would Fiji do?
Or tiny Tuvalu?
Or perhaps the Solomon Islands?

Maybe the Kiwis?
No, no, no, please
We might get stuck in the highlands

Norfolk's not fine
Far too much 'Pine'
A little too close to the bone …

Or take our chances?
Remove Pope Francis
From his golden Vatican throne?

Greenland or Iceland?
Perhaps a nice rice-land?
Either Cambodia or Vietnam?

Nah, maybe not
It'd be twice on the trot
Getting done kicking the Commo can

No time to waste
Must do it in haste
Soon we face a new poll

To get empowered
I'll ask John Howard
What he thinks is a suitable goal

The man of steel
He's got the feel
Where the battle should begin

He and George
Pulled out their swords
And into the mess we're still in …

CHARDONNAY SOCIALIST — *And Other Radio Poems*

Mars? Been there, ruined that

Within the two-yearly cycle, Mars was as close as it ever would be, so three nations fired off probes into the sky.
Broadcast August 7, 2020

What are these blokes thinking?
Sending more rockets to Mars?
Checking for previous life there
To change our ideas about planets and stars

Of course there was once people living there
Don't you see how all this went?
It was us earthlings started out there first
And then when everything was all spent

And we had turned the place into dust
And could no longer pay the rent
And the economy had collapsed
And it was a place of racial dissent

And we'd made the climate so bad
That a solution we couldn't invent
We spotted this Blue Planet nearby
And said, 'Look, it's Heaven sent!'

And promptly built some rockets
And headed over this way
And discovered a haven of grass and trees
And water and sunshine and hay

And then we set about
Turning it into our own new place
Creating the Earthly version
Of what was once the Martian Race

And so learning from experience
We settled the place with patience
And created a new environment
Of joy and peace and fragrance

And grew only what we needed
And lived within our means
And shared our crops and produce
Whether corn or wheat or beans

But gradually we all got greedy
And started drawing up borders
And turned from peace-keeping people
To marching under orders

And developing fifty shades of envy
And of other lands desirous
And ignoring other's peacefulness
Spreading hatred like a virus

And using up all our resources
And not replacing them equally
And so now we look around at our world
Viewing everything, oh so, bleakly

So now they want to inhabit Mars
As if it is something novel
But, in fact we would be returning
To our old galactic hovel

CHARDONNAY SOCIALIST *And Other Radio Poems*

I bet when their little vehicles
Start digging underground
The proof will be in the pudding
Of artefacts to be found

Under that rocky red surface
There'll be roads, buildings, paths
And coffee shops and hairdressers
And a plumber who sold claw-foot baths

And there'll be stadiums once used for footy
And rugby and netball and cricket
And torn in half, stamped into the ground
A Collingwood membership ticket

Meanwhile, we're wrecking dear Earth
And will soon need another place to serve us
Let's see what's next on the planetary map
Hmm, if I were Venus, I'd be getting nervous …

Donald out-tweets Malcolm

Malcolm Turnbull. Remember him? Early in his tenure as PM, tariffs became a big issue, particularly when Donald Trump capriciously dashed off a tweet that reverberated around the world. Broadcast March 16, 2018.

Donald said to Malcolm, 'I'm getting tough on your trade.'
Malcolm said, 'You can't do that, the bed's already made!'

Donald said, 'Too bad, I'm putting tariffs on your steel.'
Malcolm said, 'I never thought that that's the way you'd feel.

'I thought that we were friends, and brothers in arms.
'I was seduced by your haircut and your somewhat quirky charms.'

Donald said, 'Ahh, forget about those deals that we made before.
'We're gonna finish you guys off in a classic trading war.

'Gonna throw all our previous contracts back into the bin.
'Tariff fights are fun to start, and so enjoyable to win.'

The Chinese looked reflective, in their accepted style.
While plotting retribution behind the enigmatic smile.

Japan said Trump better not take this ploy much farther.
Or they'd make another trip to the waters of Pearl Harbour …

The Kiwis said. 'It doesn't matter at all how we really feel.
'We're not all that big on making cars or manufacturing steel.'

CHARDONNAY SOCIALIST *And Other Radio Poems*

The rest of the Pacific bellowed, 'We care little for such prizes.
'Our main concern right now is how far the water rises!'

Julie Bishop said, 'Hey, we must be accepting of these things!
'And, by the way, do you like my sassy new ear-rings?'

Steve Ciabo said, 'But I declared all trade could go for free.
'Then again, I guess of course, few people have heard of me ...'

Bill Shorten said, 'Dunno what to say about this change of tack.
'I thought it was all about wheeling and dealing behind everyone's back.'

'I agree,' said Tony Abbott, showing his toothy smile.
'What I'm working on is to make a comeback in a while.

'A couple of more these bad polls and Malcolm will be done
'He's all talk, no walk, there's not much pork in the bun.'

Thus it went, the conversation, going around and around.
Until Donald suddenly said, 'I'll give a little ground.

'No tariffs for the Aussies, they can stay in the black.
'But it'll cost them dearly, sometime down the track ...'

Australians all lamented, 'Why put up with all this fuss?
'Time to stake our claim, and for once just think of us.

'Put all this tariff and trade stuff back on the shelves.
'And make our aim in future to look after our-bloody-selves!'

About the author

Graeme Johnstone had a long and successful career in journalism before moving into the world of prose, poetry and musicals.

He gained an all-round grounding on a local paper in Gippsland, Victoria, before moving to Melbourne and working on business and suburban press and then being appointed Editor of the *Australasian Express* in London. In 1978, he joined Australia's biggest selling newspaper, *The Sun* in Melbourne, and is well known for writing its popular daily column, *A Place In The Sun*, entertaining 1.3 million readers over breakfast every morning.

After a stint as Editor of *Australasian Post*, Graeme and his wife Elsie established 'The Wordsmith's Shop,' which became a Bayside landmark and opened up a whole new world of writing opportunities.

Graeme's first novel, *The Playmakers*, was based on the theory that William Shakespeare did not write the plays ascribed to him. He then authored *Joan, Child of Labor*, the memoirs of groundbreaking politician Joan Child who became the Labor Party's first woman to be voted into the House of Representatives and the first woman Speaker of the House.

The novel *Lover, Husband, Father, Monster*, co-written with Elsie when they lived in Dublin for a year, chronicles the decline and tragic ending of a once optimistic marriage against the backdrop of the collapse of the Celtic Tiger. The book, written in two voices, proved so popular that Elsie and Graeme followed it up with a chilling sequel, *The Aftermath*.

Customers at The Wordsmiths began commissioning poems and songs for events such as birthdays and weddings. Between that and his long-term interest in the musical as one of the great expressions of entertainment, Graeme began working as a lyricist on projects with musician and composer Pete Sullivan. Their first major musical, *Normie*, based on the 1960s experiences of Australia's King of Pop Normie Rowe, was premiered in Melbourne.

Following the success of *Normie*, Graeme is currently working on a cabaret-style musical with a specific song theme.

About the radio program

Friday Magazine goes to air for two hours every Friday morning from 9 am on 88.3 Southern FM, a long-established and popular radio station servicing Melbourne's Bayside community.

Hosted by Graeme Johnstone, it features an Entertainment wrap-up and review by hair and beauty marketing specialist Leanne Cutler, and Finance by financial advisor Paul Goethel, along with comment, music and interviews featuring local performers, artists, politicians, sports people, authors and residents doing extraordinary things.

Graeme always starts the show after the 9 o'clock news with a poem on the pertinent subject of the week.

Southern FM has been operating successfully for 30 years, initially from a variety of locations in Moorabbin and Mentone, and from studios in the Bayside suburb of Brighton since 2015. Under the guidance of a dedicated band, currently led by station president Cameron Heyde and program manager Colin Tyrus, it has built a solid and loyal listenership via music, news, sport, health, parenting, books, interviews and a wide range of ethnic programs.

CHARDONNAY SOCIALIST　　　　*And Other Radio Poems*

More books by Graeme Johnstone

Available in both paperback or e-book via Amazon and other outlets.

OK Boomer and other radio poems
A companion book of poems to *Chardonnay Socialist*.
Now it's got a name. The resentment amongst younger generations that old geezers born after World War 2 have not only had the best of everything, but are determined to hang on to it until they reluctantly go to the grave.
This whimsical book of verse on modern life, says that despite the spawning of 'OK Boomer', the disdainful phrase designed to undermine them, they're going to!

The Playmakers
Did Shakespeare really write Shakespeare? Were there other forces at work? Another hand wielding the quill? *The Playmakers* is the first book written in the form of a novel to question the Bard's authenticity. A colourful tale of creativity, love, political chicanery, murder and a deceit that has remained with us for more than 400 years.

Joan, Child Of Labor
The engaging memoirs of ground-breaking feminist, mother, unionist, campaigner and politician Joan Child, an inspiration for all women, who became the Labor Party's first woman to be voted into the House of Representatives and the first woman Speaker of the House.

With Elsie Johnstone

Lover, Husband, Father, Monster
A trilogy

Co-written by Graeme and Elsie Johnstone and sparked by events they observed when living in Dublin for a year, *Lover, Husband, Father, Monster* chronicles the decline and tragic finale of a once loving and optimistic marriage against the backdrop of the collapse of Ireland's economic miracle, the Celtic Tiger.

Lover, Husband, Father, Monster - Book 1, Her Story
Lover, Husband, Father, Monster - Book 2, His Story
Lover, Husband, Father, Monster - Book 3, The Aftermath

www.ingramcontent.com/pod-product-compliance
Lightning Source LLC
Chambersburg PA
CBHW030301010526
44107CB00053B/1775